WEEKLY WR READER
EARLY LEARNING LIBRARY

Coyotes

Are Night Animals

by Joanne Mattern

Reading consultant: Susan Nations, M.Ed., author/literacy coach/consultant in literacy development
Science and curriculum consultant: Debra Voege, M.A., science and math curriculum resource teacher

Please visit our web site at: www.garethstevens.com
For a free color catalog describing Weekly Reader® Early Learning Library's list
of high-quality books, call 1-877-445-5824 (USA) or 1-800-387-3178 (Canada).
Weekly Reader® Early Learning Library's fax: (414) 336-0164.

Library of Congress Cataloging-in-Publication Data

Mattern, Joanne, 1963-
    Coyotes are night animals / by Joanne Mattern.
       p. cm. — (Night animals)
    Includes bibliographical references and index.
    ISBN-13: 978-0-8368-7847-9 (lib. bdg.)
    ISBN-13: 978-0-8368-7854-7 (softcover)
    1. Coyote—Juvenile literature.   I. Title.
  QL737.C22M3648   2007
  599.77'25—dc22   2006030883

This edition first published in 2007 by
Weekly Reader® Early Learning Library
A Member of the WRC Media Family of Companies
330 West Olive Street, Suite 100
Milwaukee, Wisconsin 53212 USA

Copyright © 2007 by Weekly Reader® Early Learning Library

Editor: Tea Benduhn
Art direction: Tammy West
Cover design and page layout: Scott M. Krall
Picture research: Diane Laska-Swanke

Picture credits: Cover, title page © Arthur Morris/Visuals Unlimited; p. 5 © Tom Murphy/National Geographic
Image Collection; pp. 7, 15, 17 © Thomas Kitchin & Victoria Hurst/leesonphoto; p. 9 © Randy Olson/
National Geographic Image Collection; pp. 11, 13, 19 © Tom and Pat Leeson; p. 21 John J. Mosesso/NBII

Printed in the United States of America

1 2 3 4 5 6 7 8 9 10 10 09 08 07 06

Note to Educators and Parents

Reading is such an exciting adventure for young children! They are beginning to integrate their oral language skills with written language. To encourage children along the path to early literacy, books must be colorful, engaging, and interesting; they should invite the young reader to explore both the print and the pictures.

The *Night Animals* series is designed to help children read about creatures that are active during the night. Each book explains what a different night animal does during the day, how it finds food, and how it adapts to its nocturnal life.

Each book is specially designed to support the young reader in the reading process. The familiar topics are appealing to young children and invite them to read — and reread — again and again. The full-color photographs and enhanced text further support the student during the reading process.

In addition to serving as wonderful picture books in schools, libraries, homes, and other places where children learn to love reading, these books are specifically intended to be read within an instructional guided reading group. This small group setting allows beginning readers to work with a fluent adult model as they make meaning from the text. After children develop fluency with the text and content, the books can be read independently. Children and adults alike will find these books supportive, engaging, and fun!

— Susan Nations, M.Ed., author/literacy coach/
consultant in literacy development

A scary **howl** fills the night. What animal is making that sound? It is a coyote!

Coyotes look a lot like dogs. They look like wolves, too. Coyotes, dogs, and wolves are all part of the same family of animals.

dog

coyote

Coyotes live in lots of different places. Many coyotes live in the country. Some live in the city. They live where they can find food.

Coyotes like to stay away from people. Most coyotes stay out of sight all day. During the day, they sleep.

At night, it is time to **hunt**! Coyotes are good hunters. They can see well in the dark. They can hear well, too, and they have a great sense of smell. Their senses help coyotes find **prey**.

Coyotes eat many things. Coyotes that live in the country hunt rabbits and other small animals. Sometimes, they eat eggs or fruit.

In the city, coyotes often eat garbage. They will also eat things that are not food. Some coyotes even eat shoes!

garbage

Many coyotes live and hunt in groups called **packs**. Pack members howl to talk to each other.

Did you ever hear a
coyote howl at night?
If you did, you heard
a night animal!

Glossary

garbage — trash, scraps of food, cr used things that people throw away

howl — a long, loud, sad sound

hunt — to find and kill other animals for food

packs — groups of animals that live and hunt together

prey — an animal that is hunted by another animal

senses — an animal's abilities to see, hear, smell, taste, and feel

For More Information

Books

Coyotes. Animals That Live in the Desert (series). JoAnn Early Macken (Gareth Stevens)

Coyotes. Grassland Animals (series). Patricia J. Murphy (Pebble Books)

Coyotes. What's Awake? (series). Patricia Whitehouse (Heinemann Library)

Wild Canines! Coyote. Jalma Barrett (Blackbirch Press)

Web Site

Creature Feature: Coyotes
www.nationalgeographic.com/kids/creature_feature/ 0005/coyote.html
This Web site has photos, a video, a map, and fun facts about coyotes. You can even send a coyote postcard to a friend.

Publisher's note to educators and parents: Our editors have carefully reviewed this Web site to ensure that it is suitable for children. Many Web sites change frequently, however, and we cannot guarantee that a site's future contents will continue to meet our high standards of quality and educational value. Be advised that children should be closely supervised whenever they access the Internet.

Index

About the Author

Joanne Mattern has written more than 150 books for children. She has written about unusual animals, sports, history, world cities, and many other topics. Joanne also works in her local library. She lives in New York State with her husband, three daughters, and assorted pets. She enjoys animals, music, reading, going to baseball games, and visiting schools to talk about her books.